A BOOK FOR

_____

May the smile on your face
and the smile in your heart
grow ever brighter.

Going
the Extra
Smile

GEORGE
FOREMAN

WITH JAMES LUND

Published by
THOMAS NELSON™
Since 1798

Nashville   Dallas   Mexico City   Rio De Janeiro   Beijing

Published in Nashville, TN, by Thomas Nelson. Thomas Nelson is a trademark of Thomas Nelson, Inc.

Thomas Nelson, Inc., titles may be purchased in bulk for educational, business, fundraising, or sales promotional use. For information, please email SpecialMarkets@ThomasNelson.com.

Unless otherwise noted, all scripture references are from *The King James Version of the Bible* (KJV).

Published in association with the literary agency of Mark Sweeney & Associates, Bonita Springs, Florida 34135

Designed by The DesignWorks Group, www.thedesignworksgroup.com

ISBN-10: 1-4041-0491-1
ISBN-13: 978-1-4041-0491-8

Printed in the United States of America

CONTENTS

Introduction   6

1. An Attitude of Faith   10

2. A Life-Changing Attitude   20

3. A Caring Attitude   28

4. A Positive Attitude   38

5. A Grateful Attitude   48

6. An Overcoming Attitude   56

7. An Attractive Attitude   66

8. An Encouraging Attitude   76

9. A Resilient Attitude   84

10. A Fun-Loving Attitude   94

11. An Expectant Attitude   104

12. A Generous Attitude   112

13. A Winning Attitude   122

14. A Forgiving Attitude   130

15. A Joyful Attitude   140

Conclusion   148

Notes   150

Laughter is day,
and sobriety is night;
a smile is the twilight
that hovers gently
between both, more
bewitching than either.
HENRY WARD BEECHER

Wherever I go, people look for something from me. I'll be walking down the street in Los Angeles or New York City or my hometown of Marshall, Texas, and I'll hear someone across the way yell, "George! Hey, George!" I'll wave, and then I'll break into a big smile. That's what they're looking for—the smile. When they see it, they always smile right back at me. They walk away happy, and that makes me happy.

I seem to have a reputation as a guy who's always smiling. People are used to seeing me that way, either on television or at ringside for a boxing match or when I'm just taking a walk. They expect it. And why shouldn't I smile? I enjoy life, and a happy face is the natural result of everything that's enjoyable and good in life.

A smile is the simplest thing. You work your face muscles a bit, turn up the corners of your mouth, and pretty soon you have a grin. Anyone can do it (though by the look some folks carry around, you wouldn't think so). Yet a smile is also one of the most profound things ever created. It's the beginning and the end of what you and I need most in life. It's the doorway to happiness.

You may be reading this and thinking, *That's good for you, George, but I don't have much to smile about. You don't know what I'm dealing with.* And I appreciate that. Divorce. Disease. Depression. Money troubles. Life can hit you with what feels like a knockout punch, in or out of the ring.

I've been there myself. I grew up in a poor Houston neighborhood, fought my way up to become heavyweight champion of the world, found fame and wealth—and then I lost everything. Even before that, I was lonely. I'd been through many relationships and a failed marriage. I didn't much like the person I'd become. As a boy, I sneered at everyone and stuck a bandage on my face to make people think I was tough. Almost thirty years later, I was still doing the same thing, trying to look tough. I wanted people to be afraid of me. I wanted them to think I was the meanest guy they'd ever met. In fact, I probably was—mean and miserable.

A smile is the doorway to happiness.

But then something wonderful happened, something that changed my life forever. It made me smile, and made me realize how important it is to keep on smiling. I discovered that when you start your day with a smile on your face—and even more important, with a smile in your heart—then nothing can hold you back. It's the right answer to every problem, and the key that unlocks every attitude you need to succeed in life.

I can hear you now. "George," you're saying, "that's crazy talk. A smile can't do all that. I think you've taken one too many punches on the noggin." Just keep on reading and I'll explain what I mean. I might surprise you. Before you know it, you may even find yourself smiling right along with me!

"God," I said,
"if You're real,
maybe you can use me
as something more
than a boxer."

A Smile Reveals and Helps Create an

ATTITUDE OF FAITH

It was March 18, 1977. I was lying in a hospital bed in San Juan, Puerto Rico, wearing the happiest smile of my life.

I shouldn't have been smiling at all. The night before, even though I was a heavy favorite, I'd lost a twelve-round decision in a fight with Jimmy Young. Ever since Muhammad Ali had knocked me out in a fight in Zaire, Africa, three years earlier to take the heavyweight champion title from me, I'd been training and fighting for the chance to get my title back. A victory against Young would have forced Ali to fight me again for the title.

Now that chance was gone. As I walked away from the ring after the match, I couldn't believe it.

But then something strange happened to me. I wasn't a religious man. In fact, I laughed at church people. At that point in my life, I wasn't even sure if God existed. Yet for some reason, alone on my hotel balcony a few nights before the match, I'd begun a prayer. "God," I said, "if You're real, maybe You can use me as something more than a boxer."

That evening after the fight, it seemed that God took me up on my offer. In the dressing room, I had strange thoughts of dying. A voice filled my head, saying, *You believe in God. So why are you so afraid to die?* Then I collapsed, and I felt transported to the worst place I'd ever been, a place of terrible despair and nothingness. I was sure I was dead. I saw, too late, that I'd completely missed what life was really about. I was like a boxer going down for the count, but I had one punch left. I yelled out, "I don't care if this is death. I still believe there's a God!"

At that instant, a giant hand reached down and rescued me from the void. I knew it was Him.

I opened my eyes. I was back in the dressing room, lying on the training table. My amazing spiritual experience wasn't done. The dressing room disappeared. I seemed to go on a journey where I was living the lives of other people. Then I was back on the table. I saw blood on my hands and started talking about Jesus. "He's bleeding where they crucified Him," I said to the concerned people gathered around me in the dressing room. Then I sat straight up and yelled, "Hey, Jesus Christ is coming alive in me!" I felt an incredible sense of peace and contentment.

A few moments later, a voice spoke to me: *Now, I go.* And suddenly the presence that had filled me was gone.

My doctor couldn't figure out what was "wrong" with me, so he admitted me to a San Juan hospital for observation. The next morning, I stared at the intravenous fluid tube hooked to my arm and the machine that was monitoring my heart. I remembered all the movies I'd seen where the line on the heart monitor suddenly flattened, signaling that the patient was dead. But the line on my monitor kept on jumping.

I'm alive, I thought. *That all really happened yesterday. I was dead, but now, thanks to God, I'm alive! God is* real. *Jesus is* real.

I'd never been so happy. My first genuine smile was born that day in the hospital. I couldn't believe it—God, the same God I'd doubted and mocked my whole life, had personally introduced Himself to me. He'd taken time to show that He cared about me, that He *loved* me. I'd never felt so important! That love birthed a new attitude in me—an attitude of faith. I've held on to that faith ever since.

You may be like I was, unsure about God and where, or if, He fits into your life. All I can say is that He's the real thing. You can trust Him. If you start talking to God, you're going to find out how much He loves you and how much you have to smile about.

A few months after the Jimmy Young fight, I got another jolt and another lesson on love. I was at home on my ranch in Marshall, Texas, reading a Bible. I'd never read the Bible before my encounter with God in the dressing room. Now I couldn't get enough of it. I couldn't imagine anyone wanting to know more about the Bible than I did. That day at home, I came to a verse, 1 John 4:8, that read, "He that loveth not knoweth not God; for God is love."

If you start talking to God, you're going to find out how much He loves you and how much you have to smile about.

That stopped me cold. *God is love. Wow.* More than all the other writing in the Bible before that and after that, this was what God was all about. He loves us and wants us to love each other. Without Him, we can never really understand love at all.

After I'd encountered God in Puerto Rico, I'd told everyone about it: "Hey, everybody, listen to me— God is real!" I wanted to set my brothers straight, set my mother straight, set my friends straight. But "God is love" set me straight. I began to realize who God is and how much we all need Him. Everybody's looking for love—not just the romantic kind, but the kind that settles down deep in your heart and gives you hope and peace and joy. The kind that only God can offer.

That day on my ranch, after reading that verse, my new smile got even bigger. Because everything—including a smile—starts with faith in God and His love. It's like a ball

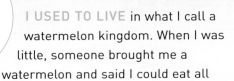

I USED TO LIVE in what I call a watermelon kingdom. When I was little, someone brought me a watermelon and said I could eat all I wanted. I ate that watermelon up, and for a while I was full. But not too much after, I was hungry again. I realized I hadn't really eaten anything.

That's how my life was too. I won the heavyweight title and everybody cheered me for a while, but then they said I couldn't beat Muhammad Ali. I felt empty. I had millions in the bank, which made me feel good for a time, but then a friend said that a girl I liked only liked me for my money. Again, empty.

It wasn't until God came into my life that I felt filled up. I'd traded in my watermelon for steak and gravy! And now, nothing can take that away.

tightly wrapped with all kinds of yarn and string, and at the core is love. Once you realize and accept how much God loves you, that gets the ball rolling, and it just keeps rolling faster, gathering up more blessings as it goes. You begin loving yourself and other people. That love leads to kindness toward other people. Out of that kindness comes forgiveness. Then, when you start forgiving people, you find peace and hope, which leads to joy. And once you have all that, that ball is rolling so fast you'd better look out, because anything can happen! But it begins with love and an attitude of faith.

Just thinking about it makes me smile.

IN THE MIDST OF DARKNESS and
the storms of life, keep your faith
and keep smiling. In the end, God is
going to bring something good from this.

I DON'T EVEN think about a retirement program
because I'm working for the Lord, for the Almighty.
And even though the Lord's pay often isn't very high,
His retirement program is, you might say, out of this
world!

The LORD is my strength and my shield; my heart trusted in him, and I am helped: therefore my heart greatly rejoiceth; and with my song will I praise him.

PSALM 28:7

Blessed is the man that endureth temptation: for when he is tried, he shall receive the crown of life, which the Lord hath promised to them that love him.

JAMES 1:12

Abraham believed God, and it was imputed unto him for righteousness: and he was called the Friend of God.

JAMES 2:23

Now the God of hope
fill you with all
joy and peace in believing,
that ye may abound in hope.

ROMANS 15:13

*Your smile is
an invitation to God
to begin working good
things into your life.*

TWO

A Smile Reveals and Helps Create a

LIFE-CHANGING ATTITUDE

I try to start every day with a smile. It isn't hard. When you've been dead like I was that night in Puerto Rico, you understand that life is so fragile. You could lose it at any moment. So when I open my eyes each morning, it's just like that morning in the hospital all those years ago. I think, *Man, I'm alive! I get another day!*

I like to get up early. That way I can see the sunrise. From my ranch, when that orange glow starts creeping over the horizon, stretching its arms across the sky, it's a beautiful sight. During those dark minutes before the sun appears, I keep checking my window, watching for it. I can't wait to see it. I'm looking for the sunshine.

Your schedule or the weather may keep you from watching the sun come up, but even in the middle of the worst snowstorm, you can still look for the sunshine. I'm talking here about attitude—about adopting a life-changing attitude. When you begin your day looking for the sunshine, it sets you up to take a new and better course for the future. You're announcing to the world, "Today is a new day!" You're in the right frame of mind to make changes.

My life sure changed after the Jimmy Young fight. When the reporters came to see me at the hospital, I smiled at them and took the time to answer their questions. They'd never seen me like that, especially after losing an important fight. They couldn't believe it.

I also remember speaking with members of my team in the days after the match, people I'd never bothered to get to know. The son of my promoter at the time was there. We started talking, and ended up laughing and telling jokes. He'd been around me plenty of times, but I'd never had a conversation with him before.

What really motivated me then, though, was my desire to get home to see my mother and my children. When I got back to Texas, I went to my mother's house and squeezed her tight. I sent for my three children, who were living with their mothers, and hugged them over and over too. "I love you," I said to each of them. "I love you, I love you, I love you."

Of course, I'd always loved my mother and my children. But for many years, the person I'd paid the most attention to was George Sr.—me. I'd focused on my career and my needs. Because I'd been distant and away from my family so much, I wondered if they had any idea how much I loved them.

After Puerto Rico, I felt like I'd been given a second chance at life. I wanted my mother and my kids to see and hear and feel my love! I decided that from then on, I was going to spend as much time with my family as I could. I was overflowing with love— the love that God showed me. That's what's driven me in all the years since to take care of my family, and to get involved in projects like the George Foreman Youth and Community Center.

And now abideth faith, hope, charity, these three: but the greatest of these is charity.

1 CORINTHIANS 13:13

Today, I still feel that love flowing through me. When I wake up and decide to put a smile on my face, it's a reminder that God is right there with me. By starting the day with Him and His love, I'm ready to accept whatever He's going to send my way.

You can do the same thing. Maybe you think it sounds corny, but I challenge you to just give it a chance. When you open your eyes and start thinking about the day ahead, try out a smile, and remind yourself that God loves you. Maybe the day before or the week before—or maybe your whole life—hasn't been what you hoped. Well, today is the day to get out of that rut. If you're willing, God is ready to walk with you and show you how to change your life. Your smile is an invitation to Him to begin working good things into your life. Try it, and I think you'll see just what I mean.

Too often we underestimate the power of a touch, a smile, a kind word, a listening ear, an honest compliment, or the smallest act of caring, all of which have the potential to turn a life around.

LEO F. BUSCAGLIA

ONE DAY I accidentally cut an "S" in my hair with a set of clippers. Nothing I did made it look better, so I finally just shaved everything off and waited for my hair to grow back. I was embarrassed to be seen in public like that, so I wore a ski hat wherever I went. One morning, though, I studied myself in the mirror. I hadn't seen that person looking back for a long time. That was me, the face I'd been born with. I said to myself, "You are healthy, you have a home and all the things you've ever dreamed of, and yet you're ashamed of yourself because you don't look like other people." I decided then to keep the "new" look, and I've been shaving my head ever since.

God made you to be the person you are, so don't try to hide it under a ski hat! Just be yourself, don't worry about what others think, and let Him take care of the rest.

Sometimes just a smile on our face can help to make this world a better place. Stand up for the things that are right. Try to talk things out instead of fight. Lend a hand when you can. Get involved, this is good. You can help to make a difference in your neighborhood.

ROBERT ALAN

Life is made up, not of great sacrifices or duties, but of little things, in which smiles and kindness, and small obligations given habitually, are what preserve the heart and secure comfort.

SIR HUMPHREY DAVY

Likewise,
I say unto you,
there is joy in the presence
of the angels of God
over one sinner
that repenteth.

LUKE 15:10

If you let
other human beings
know you care about
them, you can change
them for the better.

THREE

A Smile Reveals and Helps Create a

CARING ATTITUDE

The first time I saw Mrs. Moon, she smiled at me. I didn't know her first name—it was just "Mrs. Moon."

I was seventeen, I'd just joined the Job Corps, a national program to give troubled kids a second chance, and I'd left home for the first time—from Houston all the way to Grants Pass, Oregon.

I cried on the drive to the Houston airport, and I still wasn't sure what I was doing in Oregon on the day I met Mrs. Moon. She was a woman in her late forties, and the cafeteria cook. When I passed by in the line with my tray, she gave me that smile and, seeing how big I was compared to the other boys, scooped a little extra lunch onto my plate. Later, when she saw me getting rude with other boys in the cafeteria, she talked to me about controlling my temper.

Then, out of the hundreds of boys going through the Job Corps center, she invited me to her house for a home-cooked dinner. I still remember that meal: pot roast with gravy, potatoes, vegetables, and thick slices of bread. "I made this special for you," she said. I even got seconds!

I felt mighty lucky then, and a little confused. No one outside my family had ever treated me like this before. Mrs. Moon became like a second mother to me. When my back was hurting, she'd tell me to run hot water on it in the shower, and every month she'd invite me over to enjoy dinner with her family.

There is nothing quite as satisfying as sitting back and watching seeds of kindness bloom and grow.

I couldn't figure out why, but Mrs. Moon cared about me, and that made me start to care more about my own actions. I stopped beating up the other boys in the center (or I did it less often, anyway). I wanted to please her. I started thinking that despite all my failures, maybe I was somebody worthwhile.

I believed it even more after I transferred to the Job Corps center in Pleasanton, California. About two months after I got there, Mrs. Moon and a friend drove all the way from Grants Pass, a trip of four hundred miles, to see how I was doing. Mrs. Moon took us out to lunch at a little restaurant, asked about my back, and reminded me to stay out of fights. She told me, "George, I just want to make sure you're settled in."

WHEN I BOXED as a younger man, I balled my fist as tight as I could when I hit my opponents because I wanted to hurt them. I viewed them as animals to be hunted. My opponents weren't human beings—they were the enemy. As I stood in the ring and looked at the other fighter, I'd say to myself, *I'm going to kill him.*

When I decided to get back into the sport, I had to learn a new way to box—without hate. Many of the kids who came into my youth center wanted to be boxers. I taught them, "Never throw a punch in anger. This is an honorable sport; it's been around for thousands of years. You don't need a killer instinct to win a match."

One of my favorite verses is, "Blessed are the meek: for they shall inherit the earth" (Matthew 5:5). Not that they will *conquer* the earth, but they will *inherit* it. You don't have to destroy someone to get what you want. Do it God's way, and you'll inherit it.

That woman instilled in me something that has stayed with me ever since: If you let other human beings know you care about them, you can change them for the better. We're all a product of the people who care about us. We can change hearts and minds if we just take some of God's love and spread it around.

I've seen it happen in my own family. My grandmother lived in a one-room house in the country in East Texas. She didn't have running water, and her roof leaked. Whenever it rained and stormed, the thunder and lightning scared her. Everyone in our family decided to chip in to help her put in pipes for running water. But it didn't take me long to realize that wasn't enough. Soon after, we bought her a brand-new home, complete with a ramp for her wheelchair, a walled-in bathroom, and a king-size bed.

For years, my grandmother had told us she was only going to live a couple more years. But one day after we got that house built, she looked at me and said, "You know what? I bet I'm going to live about twenty more years now."

All it took was a little caring to change my grandmother's attitude about life. It's the same for all of us. If you share the love of Jesus and deliver it with a smile, it's like you're planting seeds of encouragement in life's garden. And believe me, there's nothing quite as satisfying as sitting back and watching those seeds of kindness bloom and grow.

I FREQUENTLY GO out of town on business. Before I leave, I'll tell Joan, "I will be the same man away from you as I am at home." Every time I go on a trip alone, I always take my wife with me—in my heart. When I pack my bags, I try to think about everything that I'll need for my journey. The most important item that I can't forget to take with me is my integrity. I won't leave home without it.

Whenever I'm away, I call Joan every day to say how much I love her. People can feel when they are loved, and when they aren't. Because Joan knows that I love God and her, she never has to worry about me being unfaithful. That's something we can both smile about.

THE BEAUTY
OF HER SMILE

MOTHER TERESA of Calcutta chose to spend her years serving some of the poorest, most wretched people on earth. Oftentimes these were very sick people whose families brought them to her so they could at least die in comfort. Every day she was surrounded by the sick, the hungry, the miserable. But she always wore a smile. She had true joy in her heart as she humbly shared the love of God with people who needed it so desperately, and her unflagging attitude continues to inspire millions around the world to seek beauty in every human life.

We shall never know
all the good
that a simple smile can do.

Every time you smile at someone, it is an action of love, a gift to that person, a beautiful thing.

Let no one ever come to you without leaving better and happier. Be the living expression of God's kindness: kindness in your face, kindness in your eyes, kindness in your smile.

Let us always meet each other with smile, for the smile is the beginning of love.

Let us not use bombs and guns to overcome the world. Let us use love and compassion. Peace begins with a smile— smile five times a day to someone you don't really want to smile at all—do it for peace. So let us radiate the peace of God and so light his light.

Smile at each other, smile at your wife, smile at your husband, smile at your children, smile at each other—it doesn't matter who it is—and that will help you to grow up in greater love for each other.

A warm smile is the universal language of kindness.

WILLIAM ARTHUR WARD

There are hundreds of languages in the world, but a smile speaks them all.

AUTHOR UNKNOWN

Remember that there is no happiness in having or in getting, but only in giving. Reach out. Share. Smile. Hug.

OG MANDINO

*Therefore
all things whatsoever
ye would that men should
do to you, do ye even so
to them: for this is the law
and the prophets.*

MATTHEW 7:12

You can find
the positive in any
situation if you make
time to look for it.

FOUR

A Smile Reveals and Helps Create a

POSITIVE ATTITUDE

I spent many years feeling lonely and angry at the world. After I found success in boxing, you would have looked at my life and thought I had it made—I had fame, money, fancy cars and homes, women. But I didn't see all that. I was too focused on my problems: people who wanted to take advantage of me, boxing opponents who stood in my way, women (there they are again).

Only after my spiritual encounter in Puerto Rico did my attitude change. I sometimes wore sunglasses after fights to keep people from seeing the nicks and swelling around my eyes. But from San Juan on, it was if I had a new pair of sunglasses, ones that gave me a fresh perspective. I discovered that you can find the positive in any situation if you make time to look for it.

Take the day in 1985 when I learned my investors had lost most of my savings and a business partner had emptied my bank account. I was bankrupt. I had to sell my Rolls Royces and find something economical that didn't burn much gasoline. (Gas was expensive then—$1.20 a gallon!)

Was I upset that my millions were gone? Of course! But I decided (after I calmed down) that I wasn't going to let it discourage me. When I went shopping for a used car to replace my fleet of fancy vehicles, I could have walked onto that lot feeling down about the cars I used to own and what my life had come to. Instead, I struck up a conversation with the salesman and learned some interesting facts about the used car business. He told me, for instance, that "we used to fix our cars up for resale, but people never believed we did it. So now we just don't bother."

The point is that I could have fallen into a pit of depression that day, but instead I drove away with new knowledge and the satisfaction that I'd made a friend. I chose to see the positive.

I know you are facing a few battles right now, because no one in this world escapes trouble. Maybe your relationship with your spouse or daughter or son is on rocky ground. Maybe you're worried about losing your job or are already out of work. Maybe a trusted friend has just let you down. I'm not saying your problems are nothing or that it's always easy to smile through tough times. But I do firmly believe that God can make good out of any situation, and that you will see that good if you watch for it.

An elderly woman once said that her favorite phrase in Scripture was "And it came to pass," which appears more than two thousand times in the Bible. That may not sound especially meaningful, but I understand what she was saying. No trial, no matter how terrible, lasts forever. Sooner or later that problem will pass. So we might as well smile and look for the positive as it passes by!

Evil lurks where disappointment lodges.

It's amazing what you can do when you see and grab hold of the positive. It naturally changes your attitude, and that positive attitude allows you to try for things that otherwise wouldn't seem possible and survive situations that otherwise look impossible. People with a positive attitude enjoy better relationships, do better at their jobs, and have an easier time handling a crisis like cancer. Sometimes they even make crazy dreams come true, like the idea of becoming heavyweight champion of the world at age forty-five!

That's why I say you should ask for that raise or take the chance of asking your spouse to forgive you or reach out to that neighbor you're afraid is going to reject you. If you approach people with the right attitude, your chances of success are that much higher. And if everything doesn't work out the way you'd hoped, at least you have the satisfaction of knowing you tried.

My attitude is to focus on the positive and ignore the negative. If I'm training for a fight and someone says to me, "George, your jab is too slow," I don't even hear it. But if someone says, "George, I think I see a way to make your jab quicker," then I'm ready to listen. It's all about attitude.

If you approach people with the right attitude, your chances of successs are that much higher.

When my kids were young, they didn't believe I'd been a heavyweight boxing champion and had my name up in lights. To them, I was just "Dad." In 1991, during my boxing comeback, I fought Evander Holyfield for the heavyweight title. I wanted to be champion—wanted it bad. I was disappointed and hurt when the three judges scored a close but unanimous victory for Holyfield after twelve rounds. I thought I'd won.

But I realized after the fight that my kids finally believed all those things I'd told them. They'd seen me in the ring. They'd seen my name in newspapers and up on city billboards. They understood now that their daddy wasn't just making up stories, that he really had been (and was again) a boxer. I reminded myself of that and smiled. It was a victory

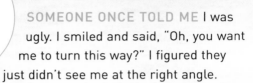

SOMEONE ONCE TOLD ME I was ugly. I smiled and said, "Oh, you want me to turn this way?" I figured they just didn't see me at the right angle. That's what I mean by a positive attitude. You can always turn a negative into a positive. Sometimes you'll even get a laugh when you do!

And we know that all things work together for good to them that love God.

ROMANS 8:28

for me. The more I thought about it, the less my defeat bothered me. And it wasn't so much later that my kids got to see me as champion again.

That's why I say to forget the negative and embrace the positive. You'll be more successful. You'll be a happier person. It'll put a smile on your face.

Don't just take my word for this. It's in the Bible too: "Whatsoever things are true, whatsoever things are honest, whatsoever things are just, whatsoever things are pure, whatsoever things are lovely, whatsoever things are of good report; if there be any virtue, and if there be any praise, think on these things" (Philippians 4:8).

I couldn't have said it better myself.

DO YOU THINK LIFE IS OVER because you've turned forty, fifty, or even sixty years of age? No way. You're just getting started! Moses was eighty years old man when God spoke to him through a burning bush. Moses received his calling from God at the right time in his life. His story is a reminder for every generation that the Lord isn't finished with you simply because you have reached a certain age. As long as you're alive, God still has a plan for your life. If you'll keep progressing and learning as you grow older, you can be more effective at sixty years of age than when you were twenty.

Few things in the world are more powerful than a positive push. A smile. A word of optimism and hope. A "you can do it" when things are tough.

RICHARD M. DEVOS

Be so strong that nothing can disturb your peace of mind. Talk health, happiness, and prosperity to every person you meet. Make all your friends feel there is something in them. Look at the sunny side of everything. Think only of the best, work only for the best, and expect only the best. Be as enthusiastic about the success of others as you are about your own. Forget the mistakes of the past and press on to the greater achievements of the future. Give everyone a smile. Spend so much time improving yourself that you have no time left to criticize others. Be too big for worry, too noble for anger, too strong for fear, and too happy to permit the presence of trouble.

CHRISTIAN D. LARSEN, CREED FOR OPTIMISTS

Count the garden by the flowers, never by the leaves that fall. Count your life with smiles and not the tears that roll.

AUTHOR UNKNOWN

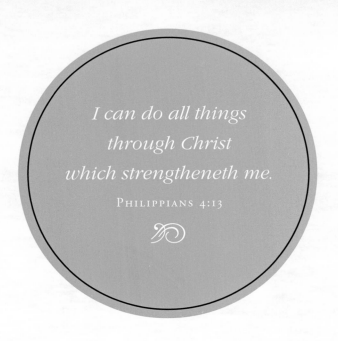

*I can do all things
through Christ
which strengtheneth me.*

PHILIPPIANS 4:13

If we have
a grateful spirit,
we begin to see
a purpose in our
temporary setbacks
and problems.

F I V E

A Smile Reveals and Helps Create a

GRATEFUL ATTITUDE

I've won a lot of big fights in my life. There was the day in 1968 when I defeated Russia's Ionas Chepulis to win the Olympic gold medal. There was my knockout of Joe Frazier in 1973 to win the world heavyweight title for the first time. And almost twenty-one years after that, there was my knockout of Michael Moorer to regain the heavyweight championship. The fight many people seem to remember most, though, is one I lost—the "Rumble in the Jungle" in 1973 against Muhammad Ali.

I was undefeated at the time, and a heavy favorite to win. But Ali covered up and took advantage of a loose top rope around the ring to deflect or avoid most of my best punches. Then in the eighth round, I was leaning his way when he caught me with a strong left-right combination. I went down, and the fight was over.

I was devastated by the defeat then, but my attitude has changed in the years since. Today, I can smile when I think about it. I'm grateful to have been part of it. I'm not grateful that I lost—no one likes to lose—but I can see how God used my defeat in so many positive ways. It helped me when I started preaching on street corners. At first, no one wanted to listen to me. To them, I was just a big guy with a shaved head. But when I started telling them, "Yeah, I'm George Foreman, the guy who fought Muhammad Ali," I soon had a crowd that stayed for hours. Soon I was telling everybody about that fight when I preached.

God also used that match to help me make an unexpected friend. I wanted nothing to do with Ali after the fight. I hated the man. And I had a million excuses for why I'd lost. But years later, after my attitude changed, I told a reporter that the best man had won. Ali read my comments, called me on the phone, and we started talking. It opened the door to a friendship. Today, I'm closer to Muhammad Ali than to any boxer I've fought.

What I'm most grateful about, though, is that losing that fight made me more open to allowing God into my life. Before, after all my victories, my attitude was, "I did all this. I beat that guy. I knocked out this guy with one punch. I made more money than that guy." But after my defeat, I was so dejected. I realized there must be more to life than winning fights and making money. It started me on the road to being ready to hear what God had to say.

The Bible says, "In every thing give thanks" (1 Thessalonians 5:18). If we have a grateful spirit, we begin to see a purpose in our temporary setbacks and problems. Are you grateful for that argument you just had with your wife? Maybe not—but maybe God can use it to make your marriage stronger. Are you thankful as a single mom that you have to uproot your kids and move to a new town? I doubt it—but maybe God has an amazing situation waiting for you.

O give thanks unto the LORD; for he is good: for his mercy endureth forever.

PSALM 136:1

I'm grateful for so many things in my life—my wife and children, my mother's guidance and love, my extended family, the opportunities I've had to reach out to people, my relationship with Jesus. Why don't you start making your own list? When you begin counting those blessings, you'll find that a smile is quick to follow.

While you're at it, try listing those moments that weren't so wonderful at the time, but they led to better things. I wasn't feeling too thankful when one of my ex-wives took two of my children to an island in the Caribbean. I didn't know how I was going to get them back. But I did—and I met

Joan, my wife of the last twenty-plus years, in the process. Today, I'm very grateful for those events!

When you were a child, your mother probably taught you to say "thank you" when you received a compliment or a gift or another helping of mashed potatoes. That lesson was about more than being polite. It's a great way to go through life—expressing and feeling gratitude for whatever comes your way. It just goes to show you: mothers still know best!

NOT TOO LONG AGO a man and his son came up to me. I recognized the man as one of my opponents from my first boxing career. "George," he said, "please tell my son that I fought you." So I did. "See?" the man said to his boy. "I told you, son." Then we talked for a while.

That meeting broke my heart. Why hadn't I made friends with this man years ago? Back then, I was all about frowning and being mean. But now I had a new friend.

Not many people get a second chance in life. I got a second chance, and I am so grateful.

MY MOTHER taught me how to be a man. A good man is only someone with a good mother.

GOD IS
ALWAYS GOOD

WHEN I DISCOVERED that most of my savings were gone, one of the first things I had to change was how I shopped. When I was rich, I didn't need to be on a budget. I bought the best that money could buy and never considered the price. Now, I couldn't do that anymore. I had to sell things that I owned just so I could buy groceries for my family.

As I pushed my shopping cart with the wobbly wheel down the grocery store aisles, I carefully searched for bargains. With so little cash in my pocket, I could only afford to buy the cheapest "no-name" brands.

I pulled generic boxes off the shelf that read "detergent" instead of "Tide"; I looked for "toilet tissue" instead of "Charmin." Before I became a Christian, if someone had brought me an inexpensive, generic item, I would have been insulted. Now, as I picked up each cut-rate product, I thanked God for the savings. Keep in mind, this is after I had been the boxing champion of the world! Now, because I had so little, it made me appreciate simple things. I was still smiling. God was still good, no matter what was—or wasn't—in my bank account.

For every creature
of God is good,
and nothing to be refused
if it be received with
thanksgiving.

1 Timothy 4:4

When you smile
in the face of
a challenge, it's like
you're telling the world,
"I'm not afraid."

SIX

A Smile Reveals and Helps Create an

OVERCOMING ATTITUDE

Have you ever had someone tell you that you weren't strong enough or smart enough to meet a challenge? Have you ever had people say you don't have what it takes?

I'll bet you have, probably many times. And if you're like me, those negative words can weigh you down faster than a pocketful of cement. The only way to answer comments like that is with a smile and an overcoming attitude.

When I decided to make my boxing comeback at the age of thirty-seven, I heard from plenty of naysayers, most of them in the media. They said I was too old. They said I was too fat (at three hundred fifteen pounds, about a hundred pounds heavier than when I'd first won the title, I *was* a bit on the hefty side). They said that after ten years away from boxing, my muscle memory for throwing a punch was gone.

Even my wife's first reaction was, "Uh-uh, don't do it, George. You're going to get killed."

But I had something none of them knew about: belief in myself. This wasn't some fantasy I'd thought up on the spur of the moment. I'd thought it through. I knew that at my age, I'd need to train harder and fight smarter than my opponents. It would take a tremendous amount of work and willpower. But I had a cause worth fighting for, which was securing stable funding for the George Foreman Youth and Community Center. I knew I had the experience and the motivation to succeed.

There will always be people who doubt you or try to stand in your way. But if you've considered the pros and cons and made a plan you believe in—whether it's for launching a new career, trying out for a play, or homeschooling your kids—then don't let those people stop you. Just give them a polite smile and go on with what you're doing.

When David got ready to fight Goliath with nothing but a slingshot, he didn't wait around for the king's soldiers to tell him it was a bad idea. He knew what he was capable of doing—and he had faith in how God had prepared him by helping him through earlier challenges—so he went out and did what needed to be done.

I've told you about the fight I lost in 1991 to Evander Holyfield. I was discouraged, and I could have stopped my comeback right then. But I knew I was capable of more. I wasn't going to quit, and I wasn't going to let down all the people (especially the middle-aged ones like me) who'd started rooting for me. When the cameras came into my dressing room after that fight, I jumped off the training table with a smile on my face. "Look," I said, "I may have lost this fight on a few points, but we *made* a point. If George Foreman can go the distance, then no matter how down you are and no matter how old you are, *you* can go the distance. So everyone grab your Geritol and let's toast. Hip-hip-hooray!"

Determination. Perseverance. Willpower. They all come from the same thing: an overcoming attitude. When you smile in the face of a challenge, it's like you're telling the world, "I'm not afraid. I'm ready for whatever comes my way." If God has allowed trials or obstacles to come into your life, my advice isn't to ask Him to take them away. Instead, ask Him to give you the strength to endure and succeed. That's what will draw you closer to Him.

The lion knows he's going to get kicked a few times, but he also knows who's going to end up with the meal.

Four years after my loss to Holyfield, and after a whole minefield full of new obstacles, I finally got another shot at the undisputed heavyweight title. It was against Michael Moorer on November 5, 1994. I was forty-five years old. Moorer was

I never ran more than three miles at a time during training. I didn't need much stamina—I always knocked opponents out in the early rounds. But I knew it would be a different story the second time around. My wife would drive me eight or ten miles, then drop me off so I could run home. I found out what athletes meant when they described getting their "second wind." I realized I had more willpower than I thought. Once I got past the initial pain, I felt I could run forever.

That's how a lot of things are in life. You might be in a situation that's uncomfortable or even painful at first, but once you push past the pain, you find your second wind—and then nothing can stop you!

a smart boxer, and as the fight went on, I knew he was winning the fight on the judges' cards. But I kept to my strategy. Even though Moorer was landing more punches, I knew that my well-placed blows were hurting him more than his were hurting me. I felt like a lion when he's carrying off a gazelle in his jaws. The lion knows he's going to get kicked a few times, but he also knows who's going to end up with the meal.

In the tenth and final round, I could see that Moorer was weakening. I gave him a left to make him think I was targeting his body. It was time to strike. I touched him a couple of times with my right, then threw a left hook with everything I had. It connected with the side of his head. A few seconds later, I threw a strong right to his forehead, and then a right to his chin. He went down, and just like that, the fight was over. I'd become the oldest heavyweight champion in the history of boxing.

The arena erupted—everyone, it seemed, had been rooting for "old George." They wanted to celebrate with me. But the first thing I did was drop to my knees for a prayer of thanks to Jesus. I couldn't have done it without Him. Then I stood up, looked around, and took it all in.

Was I smiling? You better believe it!

SETTING
A NEW COURSE

EVEN IF YOU'VE MADE A MESS out of your life, it's not too late to change directions. If you've gone down the wrong road, you can still get back on the right path. God will lead you from where you are right now, to where He wants you to be, if you'll let Him.

But be ready to start at the low end. You might think, I've been at the top. Why should I have to go back to the bottom? Because beginning at the bottom will give you a clearer perspective. You'll learn new and different ways to be successful. Starting over might even open up a completely different career for you. So, congratulate yourself if you can see the bottom. The only way you can go is up.

Hitting bottom might be the greatest thing that's ever happened to you!

I RECENTLY MET with a college football player who had been drafted by the National Football League. Newspapers were reporting that he hadn't done well on his Wonderlic test, which the NFL uses to rate an athlete's intelligence, and people were saying he wouldn't make it in the pros.

"Don't let it get you down," I told him. "You should be celebrating! Pain means you're officially in the game now. You can't be successful without overcoming some adversity. This is the greatest time in your life. Everyone is talking about you. One day, maybe ten or twenty years from now, you'll wish someone would snap some photos of you like they're doing now.

"This is your time. Celebrate it. You should be happy they're talking about you. Learn to enjoy today in spite of the critics. Keep a smile on your face. Then, when another player doesn't do well on that test, he'll remember how you handled the situation and that you didn't let it bother you."

Always look for the bright side of the situation. It's not always easy to find, but it's vital that you see it when you can.

CRITICISM COMES with success. I've seen movie stars crying because of the lies written about them in tabloids. Even if they receive an Academy Award, being smeared in a gossip magazine can steal their happiness, even before the Oscar is set on the fireplace mantel.

Don't let personal attacks determine how you feel. When you're on the bottom, people will treat you like you're on the bottom. But if you choose to see yourself on top, their hateful comments won't bother you much.

You must think better of yourself than what your unfair detractors say about you. If you're living on a higher level, when people try to hurt you, they're only hitting you on your ankles. I'm not talking about being proud; I mean you must smile and believe what God says about you instead of what others might say.

When I climbed in the ring during my comeback, the announcers often introduced me as "the former heavyweight champion." They were right in doing so, I suppose. But I refused to think of myself as the "former" champ; I focused on an image of myself as the current and future heavyweight champion.

He that overcometh
shall inherit all things,
and I will be his God,
and he shall be my son.

REVELATION 21:7

People can't help responding well to a positive person.

SEVEN

A Smile Reveals and Helps Create an

ATTRACTIVE ATTITUDE

Who would you rather spend your time with— a person who smiles and tells jokes or a person who frowns and constantly dishes out criticism? This isn't a trick question. Everyone I know would rather be around that smiling, happy person. If you think about the people you enjoy most, I bet you'll come to the same conclusion.

I don't know why it took me so long to figure that out. When I was a younger man, I wanted to have friends. But I was more focused on getting respect, and I thought I needed to beat people up to earn their respect. So I didn't smile much, and as you can imagine, I didn't make a lot of friends in those years.

Back then, after I won the Olympic gold medal, I would be waiting in line at an airport and would hear people whispering to each other. "Look over there," someone would say. "That's George Foreman. Why don't you go over and ask for his autograph?" And his friend would answer, "No, not me.

You go first." And they never would come over. They'd see the scowl on my face and be afraid of what I might say or do.

Today, it's a different story. I'll be in line for a ride at Disney World and people will turn around and say, "You're George Foreman, and you stand in line?" And I'll grin and say, "Yep, I'm standing in line right here. I'm a human being just like you." Pretty soon more people will crowd around, and we'll be talking and laughing. Some will even offer me their place in line!

If you like to shop, which store will you keep going back to? The one where the salespeople consistently smile at you.

I realize it isn't me that attracts them. It's my attitude. People are drawn to anyone who can make them smile and laugh.

I once went ten years without a television in my home. (I don't think I missed too much.) When I started my second boxing career, promoters sent me videotapes of prospective opponents, so I had to rent a VCR machine and TV to watch them. My wife came in and said, "George, you're watching television!" I said, "No, no, I'm not watching television. These are videos." But that was all the excuse she needed. She went out and bought a big-screen TV. Once it was in the house, I started watching it too.

One of the first things I noticed was that if a show got too crazy or serious, I'd skip to something else. But if a show made me laugh, I stayed with it. My favorites were reruns: *The Beverly Hillbillies, I Love Lucy, The Roy Rogers Show,* all the old comedies. Now that was good television!

When I began promoting my fights during my comeback, producers would offer me ten-second TV spots, and I remembered what I'd learned from watching television. I decided to smile and make the people watching laugh. I'd come on with a line like this: "They say I'm forty? Yeah, I'm closer to fifty than I am to forty! But I'm telling you that I'm going to be the next heavyweight champion of the world! When I get through with this guy, you're going to see that young is old and old is young!" Or I'd say to my opponent, "If I miss you with my left, and I miss you with my right, then I'm going to belly bump you!" People loved it. They'd call the network and say, "What was that all about?" They'd tune in to see what I was going to say next. And that next time, I'd be offered a twenty-second or thirty-second spot.

If you adopt an attractive attitude, it will pay off for you in all kinds of ways. It will make your relationships better with your family. It will make it easier for you to find and keep friends. You'll even see a difference in your business dealings. People can't help responding well to a positive person. I know that many, if not all, of the offers I've received to do commercials and other sponsorships are because of my smile and attitude. The surly,

EARLY IN MY PROFESSIONAL boxing career, I visited a Harlem jazz spot and saw Walt Frazier, the smooth guard for the NBA champion New York Knicks. I went over and introduced myself. "Oh, yeah," he said. I've seen you do your thing, you've seen me do mine." End of conversation. About an hour later, I saw my childhood hero, football star Jim Brown, at another table. Again, I introduced myself. This time all I got was a polite smile and quick handshake.

So that's how it's done, I thought. I was hurt, but I figured I'd just picked up a lesson in handling stardom—be cool and detached. I adopted the same approach, and it took me years to unlearn the lesson. No one wants to be around a person who acts superior. They'll feel hurt just like I did. A friendly smile beats a brush-off every time!

scowling George never got that kind of attention!

So which type of person are you—one who smiles and helps people enjoy themselves or someone who frowns and has only negative things to say? I know smiling and laughing come more easily to some people than others. I'm not always in a happy mood either. But everyone can manage the effort to put a smile on their face. It's the best way I know to become a "human magnet"—you'll be attracting people from miles around.

GREAT SMILES

A NATIONAL SURVEY ON SMILES conducted by Harris Interactive in 2003 revealed that America's favorite is a wide, toothy, ear-to-ear smile.

What makes a smile America's favorite?

• Nearly half, or 49 percent of Americans, prefer a wide, toothy smile over a mysterious grin (26 percent), close-mouthed smile (9 percent), or smirk (9 percent).

• When it comes down to which part of the smile counts most, two in five, or 40 percent of Americans, think white teeth make a person's smile attractive over 27 percent who think straight teeth are imperative.

• When asked about their own smiles, 38 percent of Americans think their teeth are the best part of their smile.

The same holds true when Americans are asked to rate their favorite celebrity smile. The survey showed that the stars whose smiles most appeal to consumers are the ones who flash big, bright, "larger-than-life" grins.

- When asked which female celebrity has the best overall smile, one out of three, or 34 percent of Americans, gave Julia Roberts the top slot. Halle Berry came in second with 22 percent, and Jennifer Lopez third with 12 percent.

- Of male celebrities, one out of four, or 23 percent, said Tom Cruise has the best overall smile, followed closely by George Clooney (19 percent) and Will Smith (15 percent).

- When asked which female teen idol has the grooviest grin, one out of three, or 32 percent of Americans, said Britney Spears has the winning smile.

- Among male teen idols, one in five, or 20 percent of Americans, thought Prince William's smile reigned supreme.

Tiger Woods scored well in a more recent survey (2006) by the Academy of Cosmetic Dentistry. The survey asked which Hollywood celebrities and world athletes had the best smile. Tiger took the top spot for best smile, male athlete. Tennis star Maria Sharapova was the winner for best smile, female athlete. The overall winners for glamorous grins, however, were Halle Berry (best smile, female celebrity) and Matthew McConaughey (best smile, male celebrity).

A smile is an inexpensive way to change your looks.

CHARLES GORDY

Wrinkles should merely indicate where smiles have been.

MARK TWAIN

A smile is the light in the window of your face that tells people you're at home.

AUTHOR UNKNOWN

I've never seen a smiling face that was not beautiful.

AUTHOR UNKNOWN

Wear a smile and have friends; wear a scowl and have wrinkles.

GEORGE ELIOT

People seldom notice old clothes if you wear a big smile.

LEE MILDON

Beauty is power; a smile is its sword.

CHARLES READE

You're never fully dressed without a smile.

MARTIN CHARNIN

*One thing
have I desired
of the LORD . . .
to behold the beauty
of the LORD, and to inquire
in his temple.*

PSALM 27:4

A few affirming words changed my whole outlook.

EIGHT

A Smile Reveals and Helps Create an

ENCOURAGING ATTITUDE

Mark Twain once said, "I can live for two months on a good compliment." Any type of encouragement, whether it's a kind word, a helping hand, or a simple smile, makes a person's day seem brighter.

When I look back on my early years, I can remember a number of times when my mother, father, or someone else encouraged me in some way. One of these was my Aunt Leola, who always seemed to see good in me. When I would visit her house, she'd notice that a light bulb was out and say, "George, would you get a light bulb and hang that for me?" I'd pull out her ladder and take care of it, and she'd say, "Oh, you're so tall. You are such a big little man." My confidence shot up as tall as her ladder. Now, as I think on those times, I realize she could have changed those bulbs herself. But she was always looking for an excuse to encourage me.

Not everyone treated me this way. My school teachers, seeing my shabby clothes, must have concluded that I would never amount to anything. They didn't want to waste time on poor students. I never seemed to be included in classroom discussions and couldn't keep up. In elementary school, I failed every subject and every grade.

At age thirteen, I was still in sixth grade, having repeated more than one year. "Some of you are not going to make it," my teacher said to our class before graduation. "Look at you. You've spent all these years just getting to this point. You're bound to spend the rest of your time in junior high." I felt crushed by those words. Right then, I gave up on learning. It was years before I began believing again that I was capable of any kind of success in a classroom.

That's how powerful words are. They can leave a mark that lasts a lifetime. You can use them to build people up or tear them down—the choice is yours.

I remember another time when someone's words had a big effect on me. I was in the Job Corps and had just started to learn about boxing. In my first competitive fight, I knocked out my opponent in the first round, then jumped around the ring, screaming with joy. This boxing thing was fun!

Sitting at ringside was another boy from the Job Corps. A couple of weeks before, we'd had a scuffle over a box of cookies. I never wanted anyone showing me up, so I'd gone to his room intending to teach him a lesson. I punched a hole through his door, but he escaped out the window. Now, as I climbed out of the ring after my first victory, our eyes met.

"Good fight, man," he said in a sincere voice. "You're going to be a heck of a boxer."

That comment turned my world upside down. My enemy had complimented me! It suddenly occurred to me that I didn't need to fight him any more, or anyone else, to prove myself. I could do my fighting in the ring and give up my bullying—and that's what I did. A few affirming words changed my whole outlook. If you think about it, you may come up with a few examples of your own of encouraging words that made a difference in your life. Those are times worth remembering.

Words can leave a mark that lasts a lifetime.

Negative words from negative people are best forgotten. Have you ever noticed that people who are mean and cruel seem to disappear? You don't want to be around them and neither does anyone else. But people who are nice, they are the folks you cherish. When you find them, you spend as much time with them as you can. And pretty soon, you start thinking you might as well leave a little "nice" in the world yourself.

That's what I was trying to do one day at a church I attended. A man had come to the church looking for his wife and children. They'd had some troubles, and he was angry that they were there. Pretty soon a police car showed up. I said, "Don't take this man to jail." I figured a church was a place to find salvation, not a jail term. But the police officers wouldn't listen to me—they said he had to go.

"Well, can I go with him?" I asked. This time the officers said okay. I hopped into the backseat with the man, stayed at the jail while he was there, and arranged for someone to get him out. We didn't talk much, but it must have made an impression. When the man got out, he patched things up with his family and started working at the church with me. When I preached on street corners, he'd come with me and give his testimony. Today, he lives with his family. We still talk on the phone. He's a good man, and a good friend. He just needed someone to encourage him during a hard time in his life.

So how about you? Are you showering the people you love most with encouragement and compliments? Or are you so full of anger, fear, and frowns that people wish you'd disappear? Take it from someone who's tried it both ways— an encouraging word combined with a smile is twice as nice!

EVERYBODY WANTS to be somebody. The thing you have to do is give them confidence to know they can. When you give a kid a dream, you give them the vision for the good person they can become and the good role they can play in our world.

I'm where I am today not because of how great I am, but because so many good people believed in me even when I didn't seem like a very good bet. My mother, my aunt, Mrs. Moon, my wife, and so many more people consistently planted seeds of encouragement that grew in my soul.

Now I want to encourage you to sow encouragement and water with kindness. And as you see others flourish in response to your care, you'll also find even more beauty growing in your own life.

Build this day on a foundation of pleasant thoughts. Never fret at any imperfections that you fear may impede your progress. Remind yourself, as often as necessary, that you are a creature of God and have the power to achieve any dream by lifting up your thoughts. You can fly when you decide that you can. Never consider yourself defeated again. Let the vision in your heart be in your life's blueprint. Smile!

OG MANDINO

They might not need me; but they might.
I'll let my head be just in sight;
A smile as small as mine might be
Precisely their necessity.

EMILY DICKINSON

I have witnessed the softening of the hardest of hearts by a simple smile.

GOLDIE HAWN

What sunshine is to flowers, smiles are to humanity. These are but trifles, to be sure; but scattered along life's pathway, the good they do is inconceivable.

JOSEPH ADDISON

*Bear ye
one another's burdens,
and so fulfill
the law of Christ.*

GALATIANS 6:2

The quality of
our lives is 10 percent
what happens to us
and 90 percent
how we respond.

A Smile Reveals and Helps Create a

RESILIENT ATTITUDE

Have you ever played with a Slinky toy? They're those metal or plastic coils that "walk" down stairs by themselves. What's interesting about them (besides how much fun they are to play with) is that no matter how much you stretch them, they always seem to snap back to their original form. They're resilient.

People seem to have a harder time being resilient. I've seen men miss their flights at the airport and look like they're going to explode. You can almost see the steam rising out of their ears! They may have been in a good mood before, but that sudden change in circumstances leaves them completely bent out of shape.

We all face adversity in life. I've had my moments: four divorces; bankruptcy; devastating losses in the boxing ring. I know you've had your moments too. But those kinds of reversals are part of life. Sooner or later, everyone meets trouble.

The quality of our lives is 10 percent what happens to us and 90 percent how we respond to what happens to us. The people who enjoy life most, and who succeed most often, get knocked down just as much as anyone else. The difference is that they smile and get right back up.

When I was young, I learned about getting back up from my mother, Nancy Ree Foreman. She was a perfect example of what it means to be resilient. She contracted tuberculosis when I was little and was away from us for nearly two years. She got so sick that she lost part of her foot. But that didn't stop her, once she got some strength back, from taking care of her seven children. My father was away more than he was around, so my mom worked two jobs, seven days a week, as a cook. She barely made enough money to feed all of us (especially me—I always seemed to be hungry), but we always got by. She was an expert at taking a single can of pork and beans and adding so much water that we thought we were getting the biggest meal ever.

My mother was a serious lady, yet there was a smile about her personality. Despite our circumstances, she was happy. She didn't want to hear us complain. If we started talking about our problems, she'd change the subject. She knew that once we started down that road, we might never find our way back. She always pointed us toward something to be happy about. That's one of the keys to a resilient attitude.

You can learn a lot about how to be resilient by watching

and getting to know people. Sometimes you'll be surprised—the ones who are smiling most are often the ones who have faced the most heartache. They've learned how to bounce back from their trials and move on to a new day.

I once met a man in California who had a series of numbers tattooed on his arm. I wondered what they meant until someone whispered to me, "He was in a German concentration camp." I couldn't imagine the terrible things he must have seen and suffered. Yet of everyone I met that day, this man had the biggest smile of all. He was enjoying life. He was resilient.

Sooner or later, everyone meets trouble.

The people who have taught me the most about being resilient are two women in my family. The first is my mother. The second is my daughter Freeda.

Not long ago, Freeda decided she wanted to be a boxer like her dad. I hated that. Boxing is too rough for men, let alone women. I didn't want my child to get hurt. I told her not to do it, but she quit her job in South Carolina and signed up with a promoting team. Then the promoters went out of business, and Freeda was in a bind.

You don't kick people when they're down—especially

your own children. I told Freeda to come back to Houston until she got things straightened out and that she could work out in the gym at our youth center. I started training her as a boxer. My plan was to train her so hard she'd want to quit. But Freeda was no quitter. One day I had her hitting a punching bag, working her hard and long. When we finally finished, I unwrapped the tape from her hands, and her knuckles were bleeding. She'd never said a word.

Sometimes happiness begins with defeat.

The time came for a fight, scheduled for four rounds. We promoted it around Houston and got lots of publicity. Freeda's opponent was a strong fighter, and the match quickly turned into a battle. She really started giving it to Freeda. After each round, when Freeda was exhausted and slumping on her stool in the corner, I thought she was done. *No, she's not coming back out now,* I'd think. But the bell would ring and there she'd be, ready to take on more.

The third round was especially rough—Freeda took some tough shots. Right after the bell came a moment I'll never forget. I wasn't working in her corner, so I walked over, leaned in, and said quietly, "Gotta use your jab."

LIFE CAN BE SERIOUS, but don't let yourself become too serious. Out of seriousness comes judgment, and judgment can take the smile out of anyone. Judgment can also lead to anger. Out of anger comes hate. And out of hate comes everything bad, all the way down to murder and war. So put away the serious and start your day with a smile.

Freeda looked up, locked her eyes on mine, and gave me a smile that will always be stuck in my memory. She understood. She'd won my respect; I was behind her 100 percent. For probably the first time, I was seeing her not just as my daughter, but also as a woman who was capable of achieving anything. Right then, that smile connected us in a way nothing else could.

Freeda went all four rounds. She lost the fight in a split decision; the judges could have scored it either way. But she earned a victory in what mattered most. She proved to herself, to me, and to everyone there that no matter what happened, life wasn't going to keep her down. She was the definition of resilient. I'd never been more proud of her.

I'm sure you have that kind of resolve in you too. If you're getting knocked around, taking punch after punch, don't give up. The bell will ring on this moment, and a new round will soon be starting. Just smile and remember that before you know it, great things will be headed your way.

I ONCE WENT TO New York City to receive an award and ran into Art Linkletter. I had been experiencing some difficulties and needed some good advice. He looked me in the eye and said, "George, I've heard about how you're helping all those kids at the George Foreman Youth Center in Houston. Just keep doing good—and good will come to you." I needed to hear those words.

The good thing is almost always the right thing. The Bible says, "Trust in the LORD, and do good" (Psalm 37:3). If I do good, then blessings will come back to me. God will make sure of it.

The men whom I have seen succeed best in life always have been cheerful and hopeful men; who went about their business with a smile on their faces; and took the changes and chances of this mortal life like men; facing rough and smooth alike as it came.

CHARLES KINGSLEY

It is easy enough to be pleasant, when life flows by like a song. But the man worth while is the one who can smile, when everything goes dead wrong. For the test of the heart is troubled, And it always comes with the years. And the smiles that is worth the praises of earth is the smile that shines through tears.

ELLA WHEELER WILCOX

Medicines may be necessary. Flowers lift the heart. But your smile is the best restorative of all.

PAM BROWN

The robbed that smiles, steals something from the thief.

WILLIAM SHAKESPEARE

In the world
ye shall have tribulation:
but be of good cheer;
I have overcome the world.

JOHN 14:33

With the right attitude, you can enjoy every moment of every day.

A Smile Reveals and Helps Create a

FUN-LOVING ATTITUDE

Two things I absolutely love to do are horseback riding and fishing. Fishing in a quiet boat in a cool stream is so relaxing. If you take my blood pressure after I've been fishing for a few hours, it'll be so low you'll think I'm the healthiest man alive. But I can't stay out in the country too long to do those things. I love to be around people too!

What do you enjoy? Music? Hiking? Movies? Travel? Whatever it is, it's important that you schedule time for that activity, for vacations and a little fun in your life. Without it, you'll get as stale as week-old bread. But I'll let you in on a secret I've learned—you don't have to save your fun for weekends and vacations. With the right attitude, you can enjoy every moment of every day.

I didn't understand that during my first boxing career. When the media people came around, I didn't want to be bothered with them. I didn't think about them having jobs—I figured they just liked to follow me around to bug me. But when I started my boxing comeback, I tried to enjoy my time with the media. Some reporters, who'd already written that I was too overweight to box again, asked if I was working out. "Sure I am," I said. "Right next to the Baskin-Robbins." Or they'd write that my opponents were pushovers and ask me, "George, people are saying you're fighting guys from the dead. What do you have to say to that?" "Well," I'd reply, "they're only saying that because it's true." And we'd all have a good laugh. I didn't want to get mad at these guys. I wanted to have fun with them.

I remember when I got into the ring to fight Gerry Cooney, a dangerous puncher, in Atlantic City, New Jersey. In the old days, I'd stare and scowl at my opponent to intimidate him. This time I gave Gerry Cooney a big smile. I wanted him to know that even though this was a boxing match and we both wanted to win, it wasn't *that* serious. But his manager didn't get the message. "Don't look at him!" I heard him say. "He's trying to psych you out! Don't look at him!" I think I was enjoying myself a lot more than the Cooney team. (I enjoyed winning the fight too.)

If you make up your mind to go into every situation with a fun-loving attitude, pretty soon it becomes a habit. You start smiling and having fun without even thinking about it. That approach can get you through the hard times

THE NIGHT BEFORE I fought Evander Holyfield for the heavyweight championship, I walked into the press room—which fighters never do—and spent time with all the reporters, talking to them, telling jokes, and posing for pictures. I was having fun and helping to promote the fight. I did lose the match, though, in a twelve-round decision.

On the night before my title bout with Michael Moorer, I was planning to do the same thing, but the fight promoter spotted me. "Oh, no!" he said. "Oh, no, not this time! You're not going to have any fun this night. You go to bed. You're going to win this one."

Bob knew what I'd done before the Holyfield fight, and he wanted me to save my energy. I was shocked, but I followed orders. Bob may have been right, since I knocked out Moorer in the tenth round to become the oldest heavyweight champion ever. Yet it was a historic weekend in more ways than one. I believe I was a witness to the first time in the history of boxing that a promoter turned a fighter away from promoting a match!

I HAVE GEORGE FOREMAN grills all over the house, and I use them to cook pasta, pineapple chicken, chili, even bread—all kinds of things. When I do, there always seems to be a crowd at my house. They say that when you're rich and famous you'll get an entourage? If you can cook, you'll have an entourage! But I love it. One of my most satisfying feelings is watching people lick their fingers clean from something I've cooked.

If you cook, they will come.

GEORGE FOREMAN

and the slow times, and add even more pleasure to the good times. I believe a sense of humor is one of God's gifts to His children. He wouldn't have provided it unless He wanted us to use it!

That fun-loving attitude does more than cheer just you up—it also brightens up the people around you. People will respond to you when you're smiling and having a good time. It blesses everybody.

You've probably heard of the George Foreman Lean Mean Fat Reducing Grilling Machine. Believe it or not, since I started promoting these grills in 1995, we've sold more than 100 million of them worldwide. That's a lot of grills! But when we started, I wasn't so sure we'd sell a hundred of them, let alone 100 million. Our sales were not that strong when I went to a studio to film a television demonstration of the grill on the QVC home shopping network.

I started my ten-minute spot in the typical way, cooking a variety of foods on different grills and talking to the camera. But then, seeing all that food spread around me, I decided to have some fun. Besides, I was hungry! While the QVC host was talking, I snuck a burger off one of the grills and started chewing. "Ooh, now this is good!" I said. I meant it too. It was so good I started reaching for more—steak, fish, sausage, cheese sandwiches, even cooked asparagus. "Wow, I burned my mouth," I said while smiling and chewing, "but it's still good!" Then I started telling jokes: "I might have lost to

Muhammad Ali, but if I'd had this grill back then, the story would have been different."

When people watched the commercial and saw me having fun and enjoying the product, the phones rang and rang. They responded to my smile and my attitude, and those grills started selling like hotcakes.

I have just as much fun in church. I enjoy preaching. Sometimes, when I really get rolling on some of my favorite passages from the Bible, I start shouting: "Yea, though I walk through the valley of the shadow of death, I will fear no evil: for thou art with me!" (Psalm 23:4). I can hear the people saying, "Here he goes. Here he goes." But I can't help myself. Shouting out the Word of God brings a smile to my face and joy to my heart. If that's not fun, I don't know what is!

I'm sure you understand what I mean. If you go through life with a smile and a fun-loving attitude, it's another way of spreading God's love. You're going to be better off, and so is everyone around you.

GIRLS SMILE
MORE THAN BOYS

A RESEARCHER AT Washington University in St. Louis has used thousands of yearbook photos to pinpoint a milestone in adolescent development—the age when girls begin smiling more often than boys.

"The greater tendency for girls and women to smile more than boys and men, at least in school yearbooks, begins between the ages of nine and twelve, is firmly rooted by age fourteen, and persists into adulthood," asserts David K. Dodd, Ph.D., the study's lead author and a senior lecturer in psychology. "Our research suggests that girls begin smiling significantly more than boys as early as the fourth grade and that this gender difference widens considerably by the time students reach high school." In kindergarten, when gender roles are still emerging, smiling for the yearbook appears to be a roughly fifty-fifty decision, although smiling girls (59 percent) slightly outnumber smiling boys (54 percent).

Babies smile an average of two hundred times a day. The average woman smiles sixty-two times a day. The average man smiles only eight.

JONATHAN B. LEVINE

He that is of a merry heart hath a continual feast.

PROVERBS 15:15

A merry heart doeth good like a medicine.

PROVERBS 17:22

If you smile when no one else is around, you really mean it.

ANDY ROONEY

A kind heart is a fountain of gladness, making everything in its vicinity freshen into smiles.

WASHINGTON IRVING

A sense of humor can help you overlook the unattractive, tolerate the unpleasant, cope with the unexpected, and smile through the unbearable.

MOSHE WALDOKS

A smile is a curve that sets everything straight.

PHYLLIS DILLER

Smile. Have you ever noticed how easily puppies make human friends? Yet all they do is wag their tails and fall over.

WALTER ANDERSON

Rejoice

evermore.

1 Thessalonians 5:16

God can take
the impossible
and turn it into
a miracle.

ELEVEN

A Smile Reveals and Helps Create an

EXPECTANT ATTITUDE

I didn't see much of my father when I was growing up. J. D. Foreman was a railroad worker who drank away most of his earnings. He and my mother were always fighting, breaking up, and getting back together again. My mother did most of the heavy lifting of raising me, and believe me, I was heavy! But I loved my dad, and he loved me.

One of my early memories of my dad is from when I was four years old. He said something to get a reaction from me, and I tried to punch him. (I was a fighter even then.) "Heavyweight champion of the world!" he shouted, raising my arm into the air. "Stronger than Jack Johnson. Hits like Jack Dempsey." I didn't know what a heavyweight champion was or who these men were, but Dad's words planted an idea in my head—that one day I would *be* somebody. I liked that. My father kept on announcing his prediction until I was a teenager, but only the Lord knew what a prophecy it truly was.

What I didn't know then, and didn't fully understand until many years later, was that God had a plan for my life. He's got one for all of us, including you. But if we're shuffling through each day, complaining about all the breaks that have gone against us, we just might miss what He has in store for us. The best way to discover the blessings God wants to give us is to go through life with our heads high and smiles on our faces. I call it an "expectant attitude."

Sometimes I'm smiling more about the future than I am about the present. I know something good is on its way.

It's so easy to get discouraged. You start to wonder if you'll ever meet the right man or woman, if you really are making a positive difference in the lives of your children, if you'll ever get out of debt or past this crisis. But God can take the impossible and turn it into a miracle. If you continue to do good, He just may use your mess to create more good than you even imagined.

When I found God in 1977, I started telling everybody I knew about Jesus. But the person who seemed least likely to respond to my new faith was my father. After all his drinking and hard years, it seemed too much to hope for. When I did bring it up with him, he didn't have much to say. I felt as if my words were bouncing off a rock.

I felt the same way a few years later when I was preaching on a street corner in Houston. A handful of people would stop to listen for a few minutes, then move on. Most of the men and women in the neighborhood that day passed by and paid no attention to me at all. My words seemed to dissolve in the air. I seemed to be wasting my energy. I could have let myself get down, but I kept on smiling and preaching. Even though I couldn't see that I was making any difference, I knew that God could create something good out of my feeble efforts.

What I didn't know that day was that lurking in the shadows beside a grocery store across the street was my dad. He'd gone to the store, and when he saw me preaching across the street, he hid in the shade and listened. He'd known me as a mean boy and a mean man. He'd known me as a famous and wealthy boxer. But he'd never seen or heard me like this, smiling and talking about God and His love to strangers on the street.

Something's happened to George, he thought. *That boy's a nice boy now.*

My dad was so curious that he came to my church at the next service, and he kept coming back. From that day forward, he never took another drink. More important and most amazing of all, he gave his life to Jesus. My dad died a believer. One of the crowning moments of my life—my dad's salvation—came about in part because I had enough faith to keep preaching God's Word on a day when no one seemed to care.

WHEN THE MEDIA said I was too old to be heavyweight champion of the world a second time, I didn't let it get me down. Instead, I got excited and said, "This is when God's going to do His work!" If I was strong, who'd get the glory but me?

Now I fall on my knees and say, "See what God did?" I'm happy I was forty-five when I regained the title. Nobody can say George did it. They have to say God did it.

The sufferings of this present time are not worthy to be compared with the glory which shall be revealed in us.

ROMANS 8:18

That's one of the big reasons why I keep smiling—I have an expectant attitude. Sometimes I'm smiling more about the future than I am about the present. I know something good is on its way.

Something good is headed your way too. Keep smiling so you don't miss it! There's just no telling what can happen when you stay faithful and keep watching for what God's going to do next.

ARE YOU A PARENT who feels as if you're doing everything right, but your children are rebelling? Maybe your kids are on drugs or are involved in immorality. You need to trust God's promise that He won't let go of them for your sake. So keep smiling and following God and praying for your children. They'll come back one day. And then you'll be able to say, "My kids used to be on drugs, but they aren't anymore. They're serving God!"

Although you might not see the profits of living wisely right now, the benefits will show up later. It may be that God will reward your faithfulness by blessing your children in an unusual way. Maybe the Lord will give your child great insights, and he or she will become a successful author, painter, or inventor. Or maybe your children will do something more "ordinary." That's okay too. Regardless, to see your kids serving God is the greatest reward you can hope for this side of heaven.

*For I know
the thoughts that I think
toward you, saith the LORD,
thoughts of peace,
and not of evil, to give you
an expected end.*

JEREMIAH 29:11

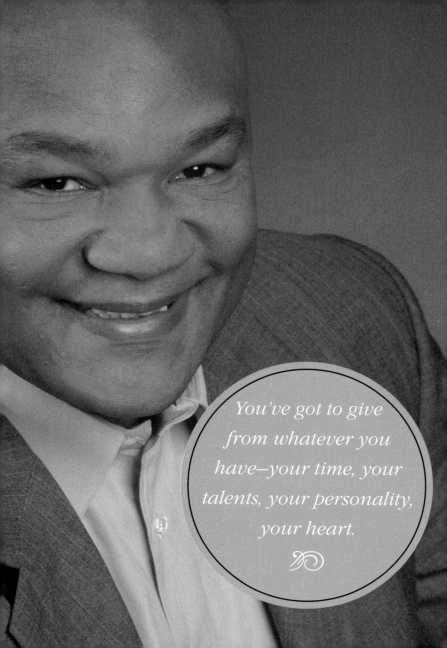

You've got to give from whatever you have—your time, your talents, your personality, your heart.

TWELVE

A Smile Reveals and Helps Create a
GENEROUS ATTITUDE

Our family didn't have much when I was growing up. We wore donated clothes that came from the restaurant where Mom worked. I remember blowing up a brown paper sack and taking that to school so other kids would think I had something for lunch. Sometimes I even rubbed the bag in grease and crumpled it up so it would look used. I didn't want people to know we didn't always have enough money for meals.

I made a lot of money during my first boxing career, and I spent a lot too. But I also saved a lot, because I always had a fear of going broke and falling back to how it was when I was little. Yet it didn't go me any good. The day came after my first retirement from boxing when I learned my financial people had mismanaged my investments and lost nearly everything. Millions of dollars I thought I had were simply gone.

I'd read in the Bible that it was more blessed to give than receive (Acts 20:35). Now I regretted that I hadn't been more generous with my money while I had it. So I made the decision to start giving out the few dollars I had left. I put my parents on a monthly salary, which I'd never done before, and I started helping out friends and other needy organizations. I said, "If I'm going to go broke, this is the way it's going to go." I began living with a generous attitude.

You can't take it with you, you know. It's like the Bible story of the rich man who kept building barns for all his crops so he could retire and take life easy (Luke 12:16–21). Then he found out he was going to die that night. All his barn-building was wasted.

In other words, what good is having all your crops in a barn—or all your money in the bank—when you die? It's a lot more fun to give it while you've got it!

Once I figured that lesson out, I did start having fun with my money. I would hand $50 to someone I knew needed a little help, and they would be so grateful: "George, thank you, you don't know what this means. Thank you!" They'd be smiling with joy, and that made me feel good. I've been handed a check for twelve million dollars before, but I got more blessing and pleasure from giving out $50 than I did from getting that big check.

You know what else? I never did go broke. I kept reaching into the cookie jar, and there was always more.

Today, I don't even worry about it. I know God wants me to give, so I keep enjoying it!

A generous attitude extends to more than your money, though. You've got to give from whatever you have—your time, your talents, your personality, your heart.

I remember one time when I had the opportunity to give, and I didn't do it. My brother Roy was teaching kids how to box at a gym in Houston. I stopped by on a day when several mothers were bringing in their sons to sign up. One of the mothers recognized me. I could tell from the look on her face that she thought a former heavyweight champ might be able to help her son stay out of trouble. But I didn't want to hear it. This wasn't too long after I'd quit boxing the first time, and at the time I wanted nothing to do with my old life.

Inasmuch as ye have done it unto one of the least of these my brethren, ye have done it unto me.

MATTHEW 25:40

A couple months later, I ran into Roy again. Something made me ask about that mother and her boy.

"That kid went to prison," Roy said. "He robbed a store with a friend. The storekeep shot the friend, so he shot the storekeep." The store, it turned out, was in Humble, Texas, only a few blocks from my home.

YOU MAY HAVE FIGURED this out already—I like to eat! I had to give up some of my favorite foods when I trained for a big fight, so I looked forward to eating them again when a match was over. In the week after the Evander Holyfield bout, my wife and I stopped at an IHOP for breakfast. My food had just arrived—the bacon was still sizzling—when a young man came up and said, "Mr. Foreman, can I have your autograph?" I eyed my pancakes. "Uh, let me wait until I finish eating," I said. "Then I'll do it." The man walked away with disappointment on his face.

That look was nothing, though, compared to the look my wife gave me. "You know," she said, "on television, you're always nice and smiling at people. Everybody thinks you're this nice guy. But if you're not going to be that, don't play that. Be real."

I realized she was right. "Hey," I called to the man across the restaurant. "Come back, come back!" He ran over and I signed my name and talked for a bit. For me, it was a small thing to share a minute with this young man, but it meant a lot to him. If you're generous with even a little of your time, you can make a big difference.

I couldn't sleep that night. I was ashamed I hadn't tried to help that boy. If I'd been a little more generous with my time, maybe he wouldn't have hurt anyone or ended up in prison.

That was the beginning of the George Foreman Youth and Community Center. I decided I needed to do something about boys who needed some direction, so I used money from my retirement fund to buy an abandoned warehouse down the block from my church, refurbish it, and outfit it with weights, a basketball court, and the boxing ring from my ranch in Marshall. Soon we had busloads of kids stopping at our gym.

My job at the center was just to give these boys some attention. If I said, "Hey, you blocked that shot" or "Keep your hands up in that ring" or "Man, that's a lot of weight," I could see them grow a little more confident. Sometimes they'd smile, and that made me smile too. I knew I was making a difference.

That's how it is when you develop a generous attitude—you begin making a difference. You start blessing others with your money and time and efforts. You become an example for others to imitate. But what's most amazing is the feeling of joy and satisfaction that comes to you. For every blessing you give out, you get blessed twice as much.

How far you go in life depends on your being tender with the young, compassionate with the aged, sympathetic with the striving, and tolerant of the weak and strong. Because some day in your life you will have been all of these.

GEORGE WASHINGTON CARVER

The man who gives little with a smile gives more than the man who gives much with a frown.

JEWISH PROVERB

Smiles are contagious, and it is okay to infect as many people as you can.

LEE L. JAMPOLSKY

A smile is something you can't give away; it always comes back to you.

AUTHOR UNKNOWN

AT A BOXING MATCH, I saw a famous singer. I loved all his music and wanted to meet him, so I moved over till I was standing near him. He saw me there, but kept turning his head. He wouldn't look at me. Finally, when he decided it was time, he turned and said, "Hey, George." He saw me standing there all that time and pretended not to see me. After that, I never bought any more of his records.

It doesn't take much to give someone a smile or a little of your time. I might be stretched out on an airplane, falling asleep, and someone will sneak up from behind and say, "Mr. Foreman, I hate to bother you, are you asleep?" I may be tired, but I'll try to wake up and give him a smile because I know it means a lot to him. When you give just a little of yourself, it can make all the difference to the person you're giving to.

A Smile Reveals & Helps Create a Generous Attitude

If you see someone without a smile, give one of yours.

AUTHOR UNKNOWN

A smile costs nothing but gives much. It enriches those who receive without making poorer those who give. It takes but a moment, but the memory of it sometimes lasts forever. None is so rich or mighty that he cannot get along without it and none is so poor that he cannot be made rich by it. Yet a smile cannot be bought, begged, borrowed, or stolen, for it is something that is of no value to anyone until it is given away. Some people are too tired to give you a smile. Give them one of yours, as none needs a smile so much as he who has no more to give.

AUTHOR UNKNOWN

The giving is the hardest part; what does it cost to add a smile?

JEAN DE LA BRUYERE

Blessed is he that
considereth the poor:
the LORD will deliver him
in time of trouble.

PSALM 41:1

*Being a winner
has little to do with
achievements and
everything to do
with attitude.*

THIRTEEN

A Smile Reveals and Helps Create a

WINNING ATTITUDE

Sometimes I hear people make a statement like this: "That guy's a winner." But I never know for sure what they mean. They could be talking about somebody's victories as an athlete or all the business deals they've made. Or they might mean that a person has accumulated enough wealth to look like a winner. This "winner" might wear fancy clothes, drive expensive cars, and live in a model home.

To me, though, being a winner has little to do with achievements and everything to do with attitude. A winning attitude starts when you look in the mirror for the first time each day. If you can smile into that mirror because you're grateful for the life God's given you, you're a winner. If you can remember and be thankful for the good things in your life, whether they're your spouse, your friends, your kids, your job, or your talents, then you're a winner.

And if you can take that attitude into the challenges of your day, then you'll stay a winner. Sure, you're not going to succeed at everything you try in life. But some people act defeated before the battle even begins. If you go into battle with a smile and a winning attitude, you're much more likely to get the result you're looking for.

That's the approach I tried to take for my boxing comeback. I knew that in many ways the odds were against me. I was an old man compared to my opponents and wasn't as quick as I'd been the first time around. But I was training hard, and I was a smarter fighter. I knew I always had a chance if I went out with the right attitude. So at the beginning of each match, I met my opponent in the ring with a big smile. Win or lose, I was going to be positive and enjoy the opportunity to box again.

"You just can't beat 'ol happy!"

I once heard a football coach talk about the difference that attitude makes. He said some of his players came to training camp and were happy to be there. They didn't necessarily have the most talent, but they enjoyed the game and just wanted the chance to show what they could do. Some other guys, including some of the team's best players, didn't want to be there. They had the ability, but they weren't that interested in training hard to be the best. That coach said, "If you have a whole team of guys that are happy, you can't beat 'em on a football field. You just can't beat 'ol happy."

That was my attitude when I started boxing again—I was going to be happy, not worried or angry. And you know what? It made me a better boxer and carried me all the way to another heavyweight title. You just can't beat 'ol happy!

A winning attitude gives you confidence. Even when you're getting bad news piled on top of more bad news— maybe you lose your job or hear a scary medical report—with the right attitude you're still in the ring, swinging away. Your opponent may hit you so hard that you're seeing a dozen guys trying to knock you out instead of just one, but if you stand your ground, pretty soon your vision clears and you can make it back to your corner for another round.

As important as all of that is, the biggest source of my confidence is the knowledge that God gets the final victory. No matter how many punches I've taken or how blurry my vision is, I keep smiling because I know He's going to make it right. I may not see it happen in the first round or second round, but I know that at the end of the fight, He's going to turn all my struggles into something good.

I'll tell you a little secret—sometimes I even smile *because* of trouble! It happens when I remember what happened with the apostle Paul. God allowed him to suffer from a painful

BUSINESS CAN BE ROUGH, a lot rougher than boxing. But in boxing or business, you don't have to squash someone to earn a victory. Everybody's got to be successful, the machinery's got to work, but you don't have to hurt people to achieve your goals. At the end of the day, if you've found some success and haven't taken advantage of anyone, then you can really smile.

LIFE ISN'T ALL ABOUT winning a boxing match or a business deal. When your kids come to you and say, "I'm sorry for what I did"—not because you told them to say they're sorry, but because they saw the error in their way—that's what winning is about. And that brings a smile to your face.

affliction, and when Paul asked for it to be taken away, the Lord told him, "My grace is sufficient for thee: for my strength is made perfect in weakness" (2 Corinthians 12:9). So Paul started being happy with his weakness, because he knew it made him rely on God, and that made him stronger than ever. It's what Paul meant when he said, "For when I am weak, then I am strong" (2 Corinthians 12:10).

See, when we have trials and call on God, that's when He really goes to work! Our weakness is His strength. If you remember that, it's easy to smile and have a winning attitude. You're always headed for victory when you line up with the ultimate Winner.

Look back, and smile at perils past.

SIR WALTER SCOTT

Some people grin and bear it; others smile and do it.

AUTHOR UNKNOWN

No matter how much madder it may make you, get out of bed forcing a smile. You may not smile because you are cheerful; but if you will force yourself to smile, you'll end up laughing. You will be cheerful because you smile. Repeated experiments prove that when man assumes the facial expressions of a given mental mood—any given mood—then that mental mood itself will follow.

KENNETH GOODE

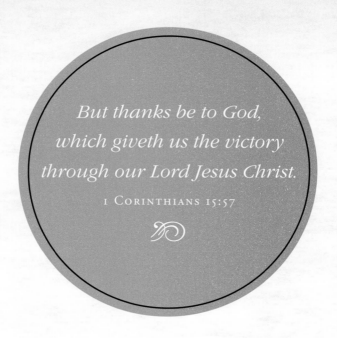

But thanks be to God,
which giveth us the victory
through our Lord Jesus Christ.

1 CORINTHIANS 15:57

That pain you're feeling is one of the main reasons why you've got to forgive.

FOURTEEN

A Smile Reveals and Helps Create a

FORGIVING ATTITUDE

I wonder if you've ever had a moment like this: You sit down in a nice restaurant for a dinner of grilled salmon, a delicious aroma rises from your meal, you're anticipating a wonderful evening, and a person who's wronged you in some way suddenly pops into your mind. Just like that, your dinner is ruined. You can't enjoy it because you keep thinking about what that person did to you.

Chances are that if it's happened once, it's happened several times. When you're driving to work. When you're leaving for a vacation. When you're going to bed. Wherever you are, that person is shadowing you. You can't rest or take pleasure in anything because your enemy is living inside your mind. When that's your situation, smiling is the last thing you want to do.

There's only one solution to this problem: forgiveness. Without it, you're headed for a life of bitterness and misery. I say that from experience, because I was there myself!

The old George was filled with anger and bitterness. When someone betrayed me or did something that I thought disrespected me, I took that in and stirred it into a stew of explosive rage. I hated those people. I hated Muhammad Ali after he won the fight in Zaire. I hated Dick Sadler, my manager, because I felt he was taking advantage of me. I hated Leroy Jackson, a friend I'd met in the Job Corps whom I'd invited to join my team as a manager. I discovered that Leroy had sold my home in California and sold all of my personal possessions there, keeping the money for himself. The gloves I wore to win the heavyweight championship against Joe Frazier were in that home. I used to dream of showing those gloves to my grandchildren. Leroy sold those along with everything else.

Back then, I actually thought about hiring a hit man to take out my enemies. I never did, but only because I couldn't figure out a way to get away with it. That's how angry and bitter I was.

But you know what caused me the most hurt during those times? It wasn't losing fights or my home or my belongings. It was the misery I put myself through by rehashing what had happened. I let those people torture me with what they'd done. I couldn't feel any pleasure or peace.

Then, after my fight with Jimmy Young and my encounter with God, it was like someone let the air out of a balloon—all that bitterness and rage just flew out of me. For the first time, I began seeing the reasons behind what people had done. I saw that these people were valuable creations of God, and I started to feel compassion for them. Most important of all, I realized that I needed to forgive them.

I'd already forgiven Leroy Young when I spotted him in a hotel lobby not long after the Jimmy Young fight. But Leroy didn't know it. We hadn't had a chance to talk. The look on his face when he saw me in the lobby was pure terror—in previous years, he'd seen me at my nastiest. He probably thought I was going to kill him (the old George would have!). I moved quickly so he couldn't get away. Then I smiled, and that smile brought back good memories of Leroy, like the time he was trying to dance (he wasn't very good) and I teased him about it, or the times back in the Job Corps when he drove me someplace to get a pastrami sandwich. You've seen time machines in the movies, but nothing can take you back in time farther or quicker than a smile and your memory.

If you want to be healed, you have to let go of the hurt.

With those thoughts in my mind, I gave Leroy a bear hug. "I want you to know that I love you, Leroy," I said. "Everything's okay. We all make mistakes. That was then, but this is now. I forgive you for everything you did to me."

Leroy was so shocked that all he could do was mumble. He couldn't believe what he was hearing. I actually got more relief from our meeting than he did, and I felt sorry for him.

My new attitude on forgiveness didn't stop with Leroy Jackson. I realized that I had other people to forgive—and others I'd hurt that I needed to ask forgiveness from. It took me two years to track down all the people I could think of, and I still think of more even today. Not everyone wants to talk to me when I call and start speaking about forgiveness, but that's okay. If I do my part, that's all I can do. The rest is up to them.

Without [forgiveness], you're headed for a life of bitterness and misery.

I can guess what you're thinking right now: "George, you don't know what he did to me!" or "My hurt is way too deep for me to ever forgive her." But that pain you're feeling is one of the main reasons why you've got to forgive. If you don't, it's like you're letting that person hurt you over and over again. You're not saying what that person did is okay. But if you want to be healed, you have to let go of the hurt.

You know this all comes right out of the Bible. God understands how important it is for us to forgive: "Even as

MY OLD TRAINER, Charley Shipes, had gotten into trouble with the law and spent some time in prison. His parole officers came to me and asked if I'd be willing to make sure Charley reported in on a regular basis. I asked my mother what she thought about it. She shocked me. "I know Charley," she said. "All he needs is another chance." I realized she was right, and I agreed to do it. Charley stayed straight and became a model citizen. Eventually, he even became a millionaire!

Sometimes a second chance is all people need to turn their lives around. You may be able to give them the boost they need by saying three words: "I forgive you."

AFTER I MET JESUS in Puerto Rico, it didn't matter what people had done to me in the past. Some people had sued me, taken me to trial, taken some of my wealth. My mother saw me laughing and talking with these people. She said, "What are you doing?" I said, "That's in the past, Mom. That's the past." She couldn't believe I could just turn the other cheek like that. I talked to her so much about forgiveness that she started believing in it too. Then she started preaching it to me!

WE ALL MAKE MISTAKES. But when we find forgiveness and put smiles back on our faces, we all find nourishment in that fantastic feeling.

Christ forgave you, so also do ye" (Colossians 3:13). A forgiving attitude is one of the best examples of His love.

Do you remember that ball of yarn I talked about in chapter one of this book—the one that has love in the middle? Love leads to kindness, which brings on forgiveness. And only after you forgive do you get to the good stuff such as peace, hope, joy, and a smile that won't stop. So if you're finding it hard to forgive, ask God to help you. You may have a barrier of bitterness around your heart, but He can climb over any obstacle. He'll bring His love to you if you give Him a chance.

FORGIVE AND LIVE

WHEN CORRIE TEN BOOM encountered a guard from the concentration camp where she and her sister had been held during World War II, he was desperate for her forgiveness. Despite all that had happened—including her sister's death—she discovered anew that Christ's love is stronger than any pain.

Lord Jesus, *I prayed*, forgive me and help me to forgive him. *I tried to smile, I struggled to raise my hand. I could not. I felt nothing, not the slightest spark of warmth or charity. And so again I breathed a silent prayer*. Jesus, *I prayed*, I cannot forgive him. Give me Your forgiveness. *As I took his hand the most incredible thing happened. From my shoulder along my arm and through my hand a current seemed to pass from me to him, while into my heart sprang a love for this stranger that almost overwhelmed me. And so I discovered that it is not on our forgiveness any more than on our goodness that the world's healing hinges, but on His. When He tells us to love our enemies, He gives, along with the command, the love itself.*

CORRIE TEN BOOM

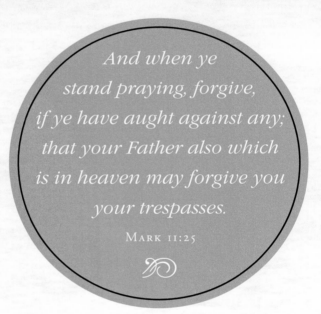

And when ye stand praying, forgive, if ye have aught against any; that your Father also which is in heaven may forgive you your trespasses.

MARK 11:25

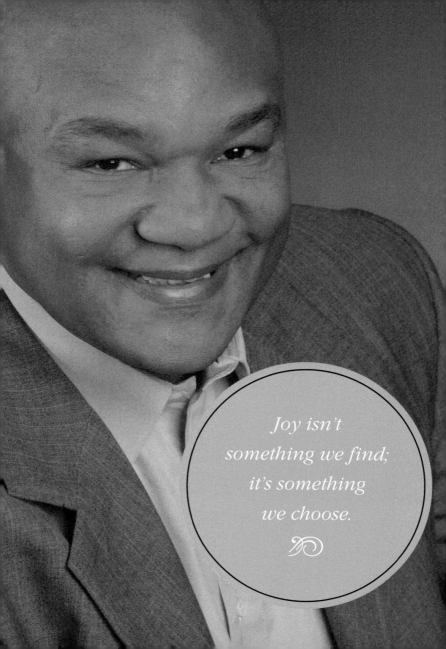

Joy isn't
something we find;
it's something
we choose.

FIFTEEN

A Smile Reveals and Helps Create a

JOYFUL ATTITUDE

For all of my life, I had a world of love and respect for my mother. The best thing about my boxing career was that it gave me a chance to buy her a new home and new car, to take care of her. She was the person who raised me and did more to make me who I am today than anyone. That's why the thing I feared most was losing her. I didn't know how I could wake up and be the same human being without my mother.

Just a few years ago, the day I dreaded arrived; my mother passed away. And believe me, it was tough. When I was alone at the cemetery, I broke down and cried. I'd agreed to preach at her funeral, and I didn't know how I was going to do it. But I could feel my mother telling me, "Boy, you make sure the people don't be grieving too hard over me." And I knew what I needed to do. I was going to smile, and we were going to celebrate.

At the service, I talked about the wonderful life my mother had lived and how she taught us to be close and not put any one of us above another. I reminded everyone of how she welcomed people into our home and made people feel at ease, saying things like, "How you doing, baby? Let me get up and fix you something to eat." I told stories about how she took a little of this and a little of that to make a meal that would satisfy a whole crowd.

By the time that service was over, everybody was smiling and remembering the good things about "Miss Nancy." Afterward, someone said to me, "George, when this happens to me, I hope I'll be able to do what you did." I knew he wasn't remembering my words so much as my appearance. I'd made the choice to smile, and that lifted everyone up.

What I discovered that day is that joy isn't something we find; it's something we choose. Even in my grief, I could make the choice to be happy and celebrate my mother's life, and the life God gives us all.

That's what I tell my children today. "Keep your smile," I say. "It will be your health. There will be better students in college, but you can be the happiest about being there. Don't let anyone beat you at this." Joy isn't an emotion. It's an attitude.

I didn't have much joy in my first boxing career. I was too busy getting mean and angry about my next opponent. A few years ago, I told someone I'd been to Jamaica for one of my fights. "I love the beaches of Jamaica," he said. "They have the most beautiful water there."

"They do?" I asked. He couldn't believe I hadn't noticed. I kicked myself for missing it.

During my boxing comeback, I was in Las Vegas to prepare for a fight. I'd been there before, but never took the time to enjoy it. This time was different. I planned to, as they say, "stop and smell the roses"—or, in my case, stop and see the sheep! I drove into the hills surrounding the city and parked for a while to watch herds of bighorn sheep moving through the mountains. I'd never seen rams like that. Then I drove on to Hoover Dam, amazed at this structure that took twenty-one thousand men and five years to build. I was enjoying the moment, grateful for these sights I'd never taken in before.

Rejoice in the Lord always: and again I say, Rejoice.

PHILIPPIANS 4:4

You don't have to be on vacation to enjoy yourself, though. Every day presents opportunities to celebrate life. You can choose joy by appreciating each moment. Life is too short to do anything else!

One of my favorite moments was when I celebrated my twentieth anniversary with my wife, Joan. After four marriages and four divorces, I couldn't believe I'd been married twenty years! To wake up smiling each day about your own life and the life and love of another human being is truly a joy. Yet even on that day, I realized that joy starts with God and His love. Once you've got that, nothing can keep you down—or stop that smile from shining through.

A while back, a man wanted to have his picture taken with me. As I was posing, the person holding the camera said, "Come on, George. Put a *real* smile on your face." The photographer thought I was just faking my big smile for the photo.

One of my sons was with me. When he heard that comment, he said, "Put a smile on his face? He doesn't know how to put a frown on his face!"

That made me smile some more. And then I laughed.

I GET E-MAIL from people all the time. Someone will write to me, "George, I'm getting married!" It's like a bomb exploding out of my computer. They're so happy about it, and that makes me happy. There's a lot to celebrate in life when you look for it.

True humor springs not more from the head than from the heart. It is not contempt; its essence is love. It issues not in laughter, but in still smiles, which lie far deeper.

THOMAS CARLYLE

THE MYSTERY
OF HER SMILE

THE MYSTERIOUS HALF-SMILE that has intrigued viewers of the *Mona Lisa* for centuries isn't really that difficult to interpret, Dutch researchers determined in 2005. She was smiling because she was happy—83 percent happy, to be exact, according to scientists from the University of Amsterdam.

Researchers scanned a reproduction of Leonardo da Vinci's masterpiece and subjected it to cutting-edge "emotion recognition" software, developed in collaboration with the University of Illinois. The result showed the painting's famous subject was 83 percent happy, 9 percent disgusted, 6 percent fearful, and 2 percent angry. She was less than 1 percent neutral, and not at all surprised.

Leonardo began work on the painting in 1503, and it now hangs in the Louvre in Paris. The work, also known as "La Gioconda," is believed to have portrayed the wife of Francesco del Giocondo. The title is a play on her husband's name, and also means "the jolly lady" in Italian.

Rejoice ye in that day, and leap for joy: for, behold, your reward is great in heaven.

LUKE 6:23

*The fruit
of the Spirit is
love, joy, peace,
long-suffering, gentleness,
goodness, faith,
meekness, temperance:
against such
there is no law.*

GALATIANS 5:22-23

By now you know I'm the kind of guy who loves to smile. I've had plenty of reasons to frown—and I'm sure you do too—but I choose to smile.

Maybe you're down right now. Maybe you've had a run of bad luck. These things happen. But a smile can help you endure and overcome.

As long as you can smile, you're not licked yet. Even if you don't feel the smile on the inside, you can at least start with a smile on the outside and let it work its way into your heart.

Someone else desperately needs the jolt of joy from your smile today. This might be the cashier at the supermarket, a colleague who's feeling overworked and underappreciated, or even someone in your own family.

The point is . . . *smile!* It makes a difference in who you are, how you see the world, and how the world sees you.

I've told you what makes me smile. Now it's your turn to remind yourself about your own smiles. As you write, it'll amaze you how much you'll find, and I bet this will be your favorite part of the book. This is your testimony to how richly you've been blessed. Enjoy!

I'm Grateful For . . .

150   GOING THE EXTRA SMILE

I'm Grateful For . . .

*Times When I've Overcome
And Lived to Smile About It*

*Times When I've Overcome
And Lived to Smile About It*

People Who Make Me Smile

People Who Make Me Smile

NOTES

Ways I Can Make My Family Smile

NOTES

Ways I Can Make My Family Smile

Times I've Made Someone Else Smile

Times I've Made Someone Else Smile

ABOUT THE AUTHOR

GEORGE FOREMAN, once boxing's heavyweight champion of the world, is best known today as an entrepreneur and philanthropist. He is a frequent speaker at events nationwide. George is an ordained minister and preaches twice a week in his church in Houston. He is the father of ten children.